GARFIELD

TREASURY 6

Jim Davis

RAVETTE PUBLISHING

This edition first published by Ravette Publishing Limited 2005.

Printed and bound in Singapore
for Ravette Publishing Limited,
Unit 3, Tristar Centre,
Star Road, Partridge Green,
West Sussex RH13 8RA

ISBN: 1 84161 229 4

GARFIELD WILL BE IN HERE ANY MINUTE TO WAKE ME FOR BREAKFAST

11-8   JIM DAVIS

HE'LL PRY MY EYE OPEN TO SEE IF I'M AWAKE

THEN HE WILL TAP DANCE ON MY HEAD

AND THEN HE'LL SIT ON MY CHEST AND BREATHE IN MY FACE UNTIL I GET UP!

OKAY! OKAY!

WHAT DID I DO?

1-3-82

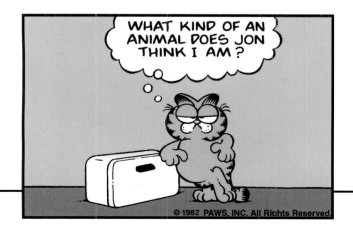

JIM DAVIS 6-20

YAWN

DID YOU EVER HAVE A TIME WHEN YOU WISH YOUR PETS COULD SPEAK?

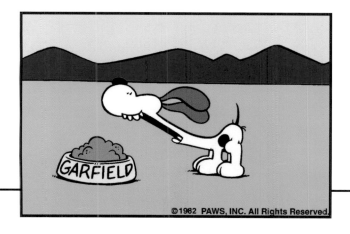

© 1983 PAWS, INC. All Rights Reserved.

JIM DAVIS 1-30

ROWR! ARRRGH!

THAT WASN'T FUNNY, GARFIELD!

FUNNY IS IN THE EYE OF THE BEHOLDER

I CAN STARE ANYTHING DOWN

UH, GARFIELD, FISH CAN'T BLINK

JIM DAVIS   2-6

NOW HE TELLS ME... NOW THAT MY EYEBALLS ARE ALL DRIED OUT

3-6

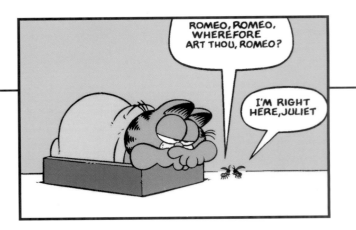

THEY SAY WE CAN VISIT HIM 2 TO 4 ON SATURDAYS

FOOD GONE! FOOD ALL GONE!

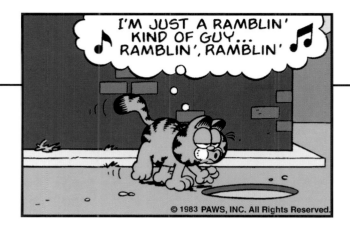

1-8-84

© 1984 PAWS, INC. All Rights Reserved.

1-22

JIM DAVIS

© 1984 PAWS, INC. All Rights Reserved.

7-8   JIM DAVIS

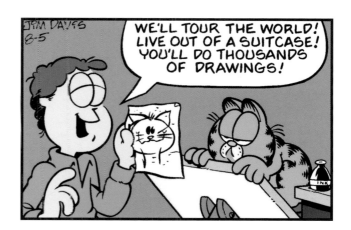

Other GARFIELD titles published by Ravette ...

Pocket Books	ISBN	Price
Below Par	1 84161 152 2	£3.50
Compute This!	1 84161 194 8	£3.50
Double Trouble	1 84161 008 9	£3.50
Eat My Dust	1 84161 098 4	£3.50
Fun in the Sun	1 84161 097 6	£3.50
Goooooal!	1 84161 037 2	£3.50
Gotcha!	1 84161 226 X	£3.50
I Don't Do Perky	1 84161 195 6	£3.50
Light Of My Life	1 85304 353 2	£3.50
Pop Star	1 84161 151 4	£3.50
S.W.A.L.K.	1 84161 225 1	£3.50
To Eat, Or Not To Eat?	1 85304 991 3	£3.50

Theme Books		
Behaving Badly	1 85304 892 5	£4.50
Cat Napping	1 84161 087 9	£4.50
Coffee Mornings	1 84161 086 0	£4.50
Creatures Great & Small	1 85304 998 0	£3.99
Entertains You	1 84161 221 9	£4.50
Healthy Living	1 85304 972 7	£3.99
Pigging Out	1 85304 893 3	£4.50
Slam Dunk!	1 84161 222 7	£4.50
Successful Living	1 85304 973 5	£3.99
The Seasons	1 85304 999 9	£3.99

2-in-1 Theme Books		
All in Good Taste	1 84161 209 X	£6.99
Easy Does It	1 84161 191 3	£6.99
Lazy Daze	1 84161 208 1	£6.99
Licensed to Thrill	1 84161 192 1	£6.99
Out For The Couch	1 84161 144 1	£6.99
The Gruesome Twosome	1 84161 143 3	£6.99

Classic Collections		ISBN	Price
Volume One		1 85304 970 0	£5.99
Volume Two		1 85304 971 9	£5.99
Volume Three		1 85304 996 4	£5.99
Volume Four		1 85304 997 2	£5.99
Volume Five		1 84161 022 4	£5.99
Volume Six		1 84161 023 2	£5.99
Volume Seven		1 84161 088 7	£5.99
Volume Eight		1 84161 089 5	£5.99
Volume Nine		1 84161 149 2	£5.99
Volume Ten		1 84161 150 6	£5.99
Volume Eleven		1 84161 175 1	£5.99
Volume Twelve		1 84161 176 X	£5.99
Volume Thirteen		1 84161 206 5	£5.99
Volume Fourteen		1 84161 207 3	£5.99
Volume Fifteen	(new)	1 84161 232 4	£5.99
Volume Sixteen	(new)	1 84161 233 2	£5.99

Little Books		
C-c-c-caffeine	1 84161 183 2	£2.50
Food 'n' Fitness	1 84161 145 X	£2.50
Laughs	1 84161 146 8	£2.50
Love 'n' Stuff	1 84161 147 6	£2.50
Surf 'n' Sun	1 84161 186 7	£2.50
The Office	1 84161 184 0	£2.50
Wit 'n' Wisdom	1 84161 148 4	£2.50
Zzzzzzz	1 84161 185 9	£2.50

Miscellaneous		
Garfield The Movie	1 84161 205 7	£7.99
Garfield 25 years of me!	1 84161 173 5	£7.99
Treasury 5	1 84161 198 0	£10.99
Treasury 4	1 84161 180 8	£10.99
Treasury 3	1 84161 142 5	£9.99

All Garfield books are available at your local bookshop or from the publisher at the address below.
Just tick the titles required and send the form with your payment and name and address details to:
RAVETTE PUBLISHING, Unit 3, Tristar Centre, Star Road, Partridge Green, West Sussex RH13 8RA
Prices and availability are subject to change without prior notice.
Please enclose a cheque or postal order made payable to Ravette Publishing
to the value of the cover price of the book and allow the following for UK p&p:-
60p for the first book + 30p for each additional book, except *Garfield Treasuries,* when please add £3.00 per copy.